BEACHED
WHALE

Learning To Swim In The New Ocean

DAREN MARTIN, PhD

Beached Whale: Learning to Swim in the New Ocean

Published by Clovercroft Publishing, Franklin, Tennessee

Cover and Interior Design by the amazing Tamyra McCartney-Burleson

Copy Edit by Lapiz Digital Services and
editor extraordinaire Valerie Johnson

Conceptual Edits by the great Tammy Kling

Illustrations "Drawrings" by the talented John Pechacek

The drawing of Dr. Martin by Madison Martin

Printed in the United States of America

978-1-942557-89-0

Dedicated to my best friend and business partner, Kevin Burgess.

Thanks for your coaching, inspiration, and amazing friendship!

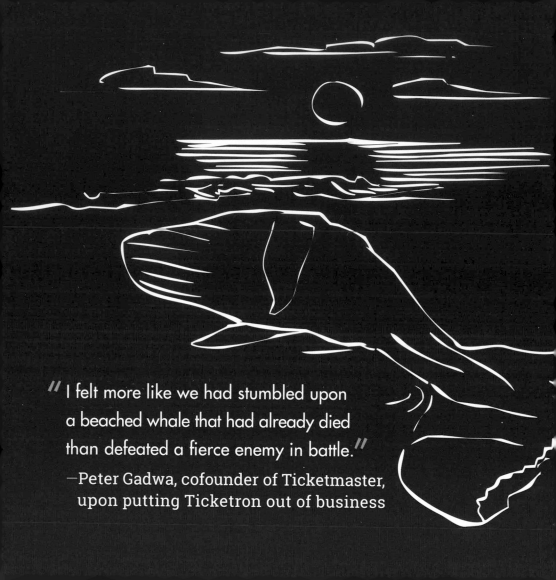

"I felt more like we had stumbled upon a beached whale that had already died than defeated a fierce enemy in battle."

—Peter Gadwa, cofounder of Ticketmaster, upon putting Ticketron out of business

"AT SOME TIME IN THE LIFE-CYCLE OF VIRTUALLY EVERY ORGANIZATION, ITS ABILITY TO SUCCEED IN SPITE OF ITSELF RUNS OUT."

—BRIER'S FIRST LAW

BEACHED WHALE

40 Tons of power and might.

To see a whale move with force and grace through the ocean depths, is beyond glorious.

Beach that same whale on a sand dune and it is a very different experience. Helpless bystanders look on aghast. They want to help what has become

"the poor creature."

The sheer size keeps the onlookers from doing what the beached whale needs most—to get it back in the water.

BEACHED COMPANIES

With all the advances in technology over the last few years, the world of business is over as we know it. Your company or brand may be in trouble. Or it may not.

Are you a trailblazer or a beached whale?

Many large companies are coasting on the fumes of past successes and dominant market shares.

But much like a beached whale, all that size and all that power are meaningless if you are beached on the sand dunes of change.

COMPANIES DON'T BEACH THEMSELVES ON PURPOSE.

The beached whale doesn't automatically decide to swim up on the shore. The whale is sick. It's lost its ability to know where it is going.

Companies that become beached whales have systemic issues long before they get beached.

WHY DIDN'T THEIR LEADERS...

SEE THE WRITING ON THE WALL

?

THIS BOOK WAS BORN
OUT OF MY EXPERIENCE observing
hundreds of corporations and cultures while
providing strategic insight to their leaders
and executives within them.

In it, I provide indicators that you may
be a "**BEACHED WHALE**" while
providing clear steps to "**UNBEACH**,"
so you can swim in the New Ocean.

—Daren Martin, Ph D

In the movie *Other People's Money*, the character played by Danny Devito makes a compelling speech to shareholders who are trying to decide whether to sell the company or try and save the company.

> *Obsolescence. We're dead alright. We're just not broke. And you know the surest way to go broke?*
>
> *Keep getting an increasing share of a shrinking market. Down the tubes. Slow but sure. You know, at one time there must've been dozens of companies making buggy whips. And I'll bet the last company around was the one that made the best g*ddamn buggy whip you ever saw. Now how would you have liked to have been a stockholder in that company?*

"

An analysis by **[Robert] Moskow** found that the top US food and beverage companies have lost an equivalent of $18 billion in market share since 2009.

'I would think of them like melting icebergs,' he says.

'Every year they became a little less relevant.'

"

—Fortune p. 63, Issue 6.1.15
The War on Big Food, Beth Kowitt

THE WORLD WE GREW UP IN IS GONE.

EVERYTHING HAS CHANGED.

And not only changed, but it's been disrupted, turned upside down, inside out, modified, altered, and robotized.

The future of work involves machines … smart machines!

Even your grandmother is on social media.

THE NEW OCEAN

The advent of the digital age has ushered in a whole new universe, and it's not just about technology.

It's about the way we work,
                where we work,
                how we work, and
                what we work on.

We used to talk about businesses that were in the red ocean (lots of competition) versus those that created and swam in a blue ocean (a unique niche they developed).

Given the changes occurring at a dizzying pace, businesses find themselves in a **BRAND NEW OCEAN.**

OLD STRATEGIES WILL NOT WORK IN THIS NEW OCEAN.

Gripped by fear of the unknown, many companies, individuals, and brands cling to the way they have always done things—like the owner of the burger joint staring longingly at the food truck across the street. Where could he have missed his opportunity? Why did his customers leave for food served out of a kitschy airstream or retrofitted van?

FEAR prevents many individuals and organizations from changing, and instead they opt to crawl into change rather than run to it.

IF THIS IS YOU OR YOUR COMPANY,
you are decidedly stuck — a beached whale.

Above illustration, from my hand drawn/written book
Whiteboard: Business Models that Inspire Action.
If you like this book, you will love *Whiteboard*!

"PURSUING INCREMENTAL IMPROVEMENT WHILE RIVALS REINVENT THE INDUSTRY IS LIKE FIDDLING WHILE ROME BURNS."

—GARY HAMEL

IS YOUR COMPANY BEACHED?

IT'S TIME TO UNBEACH
AND SWIM INTO
THE NEW OCEAN.

BEACHED

RAGING AGAINST THE MACHINE

Walk around your company and see how many Dilbert cartoons are posted on bulletin boards, in offices, or outside office doors.

This is **ALWAYS** an indicator to me that employees are raging against the bureaucracy machine. They are trying to tell their leaders something. If you have a large display of Dilbert cartoons around your office, your company is beached.

DE-DILBERT

Stop at every cubicle and ask them to share what the particular cartoon displayed means to them and how they have experienced it at your company. Ask them to share their frustrations with the company, leadership, etc.

Really listen.

Ask for a list of changes they would implement if they were able to that would make the company stronger and less bureaucratic.

Ask what you could do right now that would help them feel differently about the company.

BEACHED

When people say …

"Living the dream"

at work, it generally means they work
at a beached whale company.

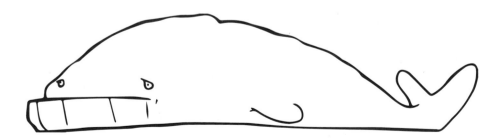

A HOUSE DIVIDED

Whether you're an entrepreneur who owns a company or an executive or leader who works in one, you can hear the culture in the words people use. Listen to how many times the following phrases are used around your company…

- Stepping on toes
- Choose your battles
- Don't buck the system
- Do you want to die on that hill?
- They…
- The powers that be
- Dead in the water
- Don't rock the boat

When I frequently hear these phrases around a company, I can be certain the company is beached. They describe a company where playing politics is the key to success. They describe a company where ideas are weighed based on who has the power and authority to squish them, instead of on the merits of the idea. They reflect a company where different parts of the company are "at war" for resources and attention.

27

UNBEACH

COME TOGETHER, RIGHT NOW

Examine what is at the heart of this "we are at war with each other" or "what's the point?" mentality within your company and address it.

Look at the management structure and philosophy and consider how it exacerbates this "house divided against itself" philosophy.

Find the origination and heart of this thinking and put a stake through it—with malice.

Wage War on division and commit to creating a company of progressive thinkers who love what they do and do what they love—be the change.

BEACHED

THE

THEM

THEY

PRONOUN PERIL

In Beached Whale companies, other departments and parts of the company are referred to as "**The**," and management is referred to as "**They**."

Customers, vendors, and consultants are viewed as outside entities instead of as partners and important parts of the team. This indicates a total disconnect.

" THE IT department... "

" THEY don't want us to do it that way... "

" THE audit group told us we couldn't... "

" THE customers don't... "

UNBEACH

" **Words are currency!** " —Tammy Kling

OUR

There is power in words.

Words become the culture individuals and teams revolve around.
What words are you using?

Insist on using the words "Our" instead of "The" when referring to
other parts of the company including customers and vendors.

" OUR IT department... "

" OUR management team doesn't want
us to do it that way... "

" OUR audit partners told us we couldn't..."

" OUR customers don't... "

BEACHED

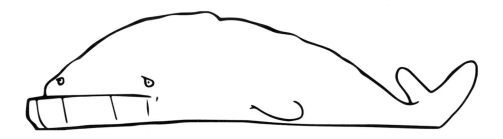

BUNKERED SILOS

In BW (Beached Whale) Companies, silos are everywhere, and they are well protected. Teams talk about other departments and functions with disdain, and they bemoan how ineffective they are or how difficult they are to work with. The left hand clearly has no idea what the right hand is doing. In fact, the two hands are often working at cross-purposes with each other.

The business is not viewed as an interconnected enterprise but as a bunch of bits and pieces cobbled together. Success is measured locally by what our group did, not by the success of the overall outcome.

This is relational death within an organization, a family, or an individual life. Any individual has many moving cells, parts, and organs that make up the whole, yet one is just as important and necessary as the other to function. Healthy companies, individuals, and relationships are in synch holistically. They function as one.

UNBEACH

ELIMINATE SILOS

Enterprise, Enterprise, Enterprise!

Communicate and collaborate so team members view the company authentically as one entity and not a series of castles. Recognize that every part is interdependent on the other parts. Create opportunities for parts and pieces of the company to interact and collaborate with other parts.

Eliminate all "us/them" talk and attitudes and insist on a strong collective "we." View the company as one team that wins or loses together rather than multiple teams working at odds with each other.

Our wins are your wins. Your losses are ours too.

Healthy companies have a culture of synchronicity.

BEACHED

ALIENATE OUTSIDERS WITH A CLASS MENTALITY

I heard a C-level executive refer to consultants as **"blood sucking leaches."**

It was not surprising that at this companies' plants there were signs on the bathroom door reading **"Employees Only! No Contractors."** When you foster this kind of mentality about any one group, it translates into every other group.

A house divided against itself cannot stand.
When BW companies view the different functions of the company as suspect, then on a sand dune they will sit.

UNBEACH

ONE CLASS

Build character as an individual asset within the organization.

Treat everyone involved in the company including customers, hourly workers, managers, vendors, shareholders, and consultants with the same level of respect and care.

Recognize that all the moving parts are interdependent, and no one part is more important than another.

Create awards that recognize giving and inter connectedness, and build a culture of cohesiveness where leaders at every level are celebrated.

Recognize there are only WE and US.

BEACHED

"*BEACH*" **ABOUT NOT BEING ABLE TO GET** "*THESE KIDS*" **TO WORK**

You are right... Today's emerging workforces do not want to keep their heads down and plug along, working for the "man" until they put in their 20 years and maybe make partner. They're much smarter than that.

They're also not keen on working tedious 60-hour weeks. And, yes, you are right. Many Millennials would like to advance and be given authority in very short order.

When you groan about the good old days and bemoan how lazy the current workforce is, you exacerbate the problem and miss the supreme opportunities that are present with this new generation.

UNBEACH

HUG A MILLENNIAL

Dispel the myths.

Rather than griping about the current emerging workforce not working in the same ways as previous generations, figure out what Millennials want and how they thrive. Chances are, this generations' values and way of operating are more conducive to the current direction anyway.

How do you think they developed those ideas in the first place? Video games taught them to move fast, have short attention spans with immediate feedback and results, the power of gaming, and a thirst for stimulation. In addition, they actually care about social causes, impacting the world for good, preserving our planet, enjoying life, and possessing many other positive values.

BEACHED

Defense Contractor VP : *"Social media is a fad."*

Me : *"Really? Let me ask you something. Who is more aggressively pursuing social media as a tool, the Department of Defense or your company?"*

Defense Contractor VP : Two-second pause, *"The DOD."*

Me : *"We are not having this conversation!"*

"ACCESS DENIED"

BWs do their best to cut off access to the outside world. Particularly, the "evil world" of social media, which includes things like YouTube, Facebook, blogs, and more.

This is done presumably to keep people from wasting time surfing the Internet. LinkedIn tends to retain special access status because it's viewed as being "business appropriate." By shutting off access, you fully acknowledge you missed the memo that communication has shifted.

When you block access, you are also limiting networking opportunities, learning opportunities, research capabilities, and idea sparkers.

OPEN THE DOOR

There is a wealth of information online. **Use it robustly rather than limiting it.** Connect your organization and get them talking. Look for ways to idea-share, connect, and learn.

At one company, I started "Ted Tuesdays." Whoever was interested would bring their lunch and watch a random Ted Talk and discuss their responses to it and how it may impact their business.

Encourage robust communication within the company by providing tools for instant messaging or create an internal Facebook style app where people can post statuses, share news and information, and even gather socially.

Use social media to empower yourself, your employees, and teams. Share information with clients, do your due diligence, develop online leadership training, and encourage ideation.

49

NEWSFLASH:

If you have employees spending large amounts of their day
on Facebook, the problem is NOT Facebook.

I call this double standard that
demonizes technology:

"OLD MAN-
ISM."

THE NEW
WATER
COOLER

In an attempt to connect a very disjointed organization, we implemented a Twitter-style feed on the main internal company page. Anybody could post anything at any time. Others would see it in their feed.

There were a number of business posts asking for information and resources. There were also a number of "frivolous" posts like, "My office is cold!" or "Who wants to go to lunch?" This outraged many managers who saw it as a complete waste of time. Some even threatened their employees saying, "If I see you posting on there, it means you don't have enough to do."

I reasoned that it was an electronic water cooler, and the posts took a fraction of the time they would have consumed if they stopped and chatted in the hallway or after a meeting. Which takes longer, to post "My office is cold!" or yacking about your recent vacation in the hallway?

BEACHED

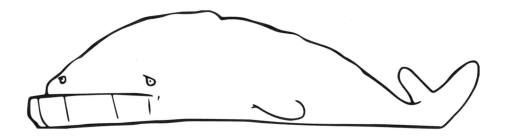

KEEP CUSTOMERS AT A DISTANCE

BW companies keep customers in the dark. They don't want them to know how the sausage is made. They keep the kimono tight. After all, if customers knew what was really going on, they may want to have input or worse yet, stop doing business with us. "What we do behind the curtain is our business" is a proclamation of BW companies.

BW companies monitor what customers are saying about them in social media but dismiss negative feedback or respond defensively. They then try to shut down conversations that are not in their favor.

UNBEACH

COLLABORATE, CO-CREATE, & ADVERTISE TRANSPARENCY

Treat customers as partners. They are one of your best resources for figuring out what to do next and how to do it. They are an amazing set of eyes and ears who are all too eager to share brilliant gems with you about your products and offerings.

It doesn't matter if you're an individual entrepreneur, a CEO, or an intrapreneur inside a major organization—transparency works. It's attractive and alluring. It says, "I have nothing to hide."

The good news, customers are talking about you. The bad news, customers are talking about you. And in today's world, they have a MEGAPHONE. View social media as a huge opportunity for feedback. Have conversations, not debates. Respond to criticism with humility and thankfulness. Remember, you have a chance to address it and do something about it.

Open multiple channels to connect openly with your customers and partners. When you advertise transparency, everyone knows the door is open, and you're far more likely to be approached with complaints before they turn into problems.

I had appetizers and drinks at The Rooftop Lounge in Laguna Beach. They displayed a number where you could anonymously text feedback directly to the manager. I used it to give Brooke, my server, praise for her good energy and excellent service. I received a prompt response thanking me and telling me they would pass it along.

(Wyoming's Rib and Chop House in Cheyenne has the same thing.)

WELL DONE!

By the way, if you don't want people to see how the "sausage is made," maybe it is time for a new process for making the sausage!

TORTOISE & THE HARE

The tortoise and the hare set out to run a race. The hare was confident and gloating because, after all, he was faster, nimbler, and knew the route they were going to run very well! Stakes were high, but the hare's confidence grew when he saw the short, stubby legs of the tortoise.

The gun went off. The hare blazed ahead and looked back to see the tortoise barely moving. "Ha," he scoffed, "victory is mine!" Back at the starting line, the tortoise was checking his route via his smart phone for possible encumbrances. He checked the subway options and timed his route for maximum speed. Heading to the closest station, he also confirmed food options along the way in case he needed energy. He alerted his massive social network to his intended route and indicated that all help would be appreciated.

He received quick responses with promises of support ranging from refreshments en route to the expediting of passage from a subway worker. Knowing the finish line was several blocks from his disembarkment point of the subway, he deftly ordered an Uber car to be waiting to drive him across the finish line. The pictures he posted along his journey were well "Liked," and there was a large crowd to cheer him as he crossed the finish line.

The hare ran like crazy. Of course, he did not let his guard down nor take a nap. A lot was at stake, and he gave it all he had. When he arrived at the finish line, huffing and puffing from exhaustion and effort, he found a relaxed tortoise drinking a Mai Tai in an easy chair (both provided by strangers within his social network). Evidently, he had been there quite a while!

"IN THE NEW WORLD IT IS NOT THE BIG FISH WHICH EATS THE SMALL FISH, IT'S THE FAST FISH WHICH EATS THE SLOW FISH."

—KLAUS SCHWAB

BEACHED

DRAG KINGS

Beached companies are SLOW.
They think slow, they move slowly,
and they are slow to act on new ideas.

Everything happens by committee and has to be run through some convoluted "checks and balances" process. Consequently, things take way longer than they should, and many great ideas and changes never see the light of day.

UNBEACH

ACCELERATE

Pick up the pace.

Speed up.

Eliminate anything that
creates unnecessary work.

Eliminate anything that prolongs
the process unnecessarily.

Eliminate anything that creates
friction to speed and movement.

Become agile and quick.

BEACHED

REJECT NEW IDEAS AND THINKING

At one company, I witnessed what I call the innovation gauntlet. When an employee had an idea, they went through an arduous application and submission process. If the idea was selected for review, they would go before a daunting committee of senior level managers that would pick the idea apart, describing everything they didn't like about it. If they were one of the very few selected for advancement, they had survived the process and were permitted to proceed with caution.

Chances are you've also seen individuals who reject innovation. If you have ever had an idea shot down by a Negative Nelly or a Disaster Dan, you understand the way it feels. Many people simply react out of a place of fear and protection versus hope and inspiration.

UNBEACH

BONUS: *Google how 3M went from being the Minnesota Manufacturing and Mining Company to being synonymous with office products.*

FOSTER INNOVATION AND CREATIVITY

Cultivate a creative culture by offering an innovation award! Celebrate the birth of new ideas. Build an idea think tank, a room where ideas can flow, where whiteboards grace the walls, and where individuals can collaborate. Let everyone know that innovation is welcomed and celebrated.

Contrast the beached innovation process with Google's approach. Google has a philosophy of vetting ideas late. At Google, if you have an idea or innovation, they support you and cheer you on to see where the idea goes. If it becomes apparent that the idea is not going to accomplish the desired result, they look for what they can borrow from the idea to use in other places.

Hint: *It was because one innovative employee persevered in spite of multiple attempts to shut down his "not our core product" pursuits.*

BEACHED

RELY ON HUNCHES, EDUCATED GUESSES, AND INSTINCT

BWs guess at what is going on in their business and tweak and adjust accordingly. They consider it an art form developed from a combination of tribal knowledge and experience. They speculate about what the problem is, try to copy what their competitor is doing, prognosticate about what customers really want, and hire people based on their gut instincts.

THE PROBLEM?
Many times they are dead wrong.

"BENCH–MARKING IS STUPID!"

–TOM PETERS

RUSSIAN ROULETTE

We ran numbers on the call center for a small company.

When answering the phone:

{ One individual had a **70% CLOSE RATE.** }   { Another individual had a **30% CLOSE RATE.** }

One person's close rate was double that of the person sitting next to her. In essence, they were playing Russian roulette with who picked up the phone.

Before running the numbers, their manager would have claimed the two individuals were equally effective.

UNBEACH

COMPETE WITH ANALYTICS

Today's world is all about the numbers. Big data, little data, it doesn't matter. You need it to know what is really going on.

The only thing worse than no data is bad data.

Watch the movie Money Ball. If data can help a Major League Baseball team win a World Series, it can help your business win more business. Stop guessing at what is going on. Capture and examine data for the real story.

Develop a quality system for capturing and analyzing meaningful data and information.

BEACHED

VALUE HARD WORK AND LONG HOURS

BWs have a Mom and Pop work ethic. It harkens back to the farm day work ethic when farmers rose with the chickens and collapsed in bed after a 14-hour day.

Executives walk the halls to see who is at work at the crack of dawn or who leaves before the sun sets. Promotions are given based on perception of long hours worked and a person's willingness to give up countless weekends for the cause.

It's a badge of honor to have accrued weeks and weeks of unused vacation days. When someone says they are taking vacation or a day off, the snarky response is,

" I wish I were able to do that."

UNBEACH

I tell people I hire,

" I pay for outcomes, not activity. "

VALUE PRODUCTION AND PERFORMANCE

Research does not support the value of a consistent 70-hour work-week. We are wired to work well when we rest well. I sometimes tell companies they don't have enough lazy people working there.

Why do I say this? Lazy people figure out faster, more efficient ways to get the work done. I am convinced that behind every efficient invention (shovel, wheel, ladder, etc.) was a lazy person saying, "I am sick of doing this the hard way!" Quit measuring hours worked and start evaluating outcomes accomplished, progresses made, and innovations and advances implemented.

Frown on people who refuse to recreate because perpetual burnout stifles creativity, innovation, and new ideas. Value actual performance over the perception of performance.

NO REST IN A PLACE OF RESPITE

I went on my morning powerwalk (inspired by the great Tony Robbins) where I express gratitude, envision my future, and take time to meditate. I settled onto a bench in the beautiful fountain plaza built next to an office building, an oasis in the heart of downtown Dallas. The beautiful fountains, water falls, sound of water, and gorgeous trees create a perfect place for thoughtful meditation in the middle of the city.

I positioned myself on one of the benches in the full Lotus position with legs crossed, right hand in left hand with thumbs touching forming an arc and began a moment of reflection and meditation. After a few minutes the building's security guard interrupted me…

Security Guard: "Excuse me!"

Me: "Good morning!"

Security Guard: "This is private property, and the owners of this building ask that you not put your feet on the furniture."
(Technically, they were in my lap.)

Me: "Oh, I'm sorry."

Security Guard: "Also, you cannot appear like you are sleeping."

Me: "Actually, I was meditating."

Security Guard: "That may be but it can't look like you're sleeping. If you know anything about corporate America, you know that there are certain expectations."

Me: (Laughing) "I am going to change corporate America."

Security Guard: "I tell young people, 'If you want to change corporate America, go to college, get a degree, make a lot of money, come back and buy the building, then you can change corporate America.'"

I complied, told him thanks, and spent the next five minutes laughing to myself at the irony. The builders of this amazing spot envisioned a place to receive respite in the middle of the hustle and bustle of work and life, yet this is the one thing not allowed here.

BEACHED

THAT WASTE OF TIME HIPPY DIPPY STUFF

Mindfulness and meditation are considered wastes of time by corporate America.

You get ahead as a company by go, go, going.

You do not get ahead by staring off into space for prolonged periods of time or by silent reflection.

That is time wasted you could spend answering email and other tasks.

UNBEACH

TIME TO
ENLIGHTEN UP

What do...
- Bill Gates
- Steve Jobs
- Albert Einstein

- Benjamin Franklin
- Seth Godin
- Tim Ferris

All have in common?

THEY ALL VALUE(D) AND PRACTICE(D) SOME TYPE OF MEDITATIVE PRACTICE.

Provide time and training for your team to create space in their day for meditation and mindfulness. Meditation doesn't have to be what hippies do. Meditation and mindfulness are higher levels of self-awareness, time alone, a literal block of time on the calendar to think, or just be—versus do.

Do ideas thrive
at your company
or perish?

Above illustration, from my hand drawn/written book
Whiteboard: *Business Models that Inspire Action.*

THINKERS THINK

Create margin time on your calendar and encourage the same with your employees and team.

Still don't believe the value of meditation and mindfulness?

For more on the topic, check out Matt Tenney's book,

The Mindfulness Edge: *How to Rewire Your Brain for Leadership and Personal Excellence Without Adding to Your Schedule.*

Also, read anything by Jon Kabat-Zin and Thich Nhat Hanh.

BEACHED

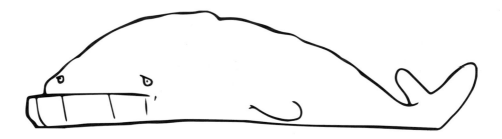

SHOOT THE MESSENGER

BW companies are into messenger shooting.

In a BW company, you are stoned for telling the emperor he is not wearing any clothes. Senior management dismisses negative input from those "down the chain" as whining and complaining. There is a "let them eat cake" attitude from senior management regarding the concerns of the "rank and file."

Consultants and many of the rank and file are well aware of breakdowns and shortcomings that are impeding business. In spite of this, they are seldom listened to or worse yet, are viewed as complainers because they don't buy into the rosy picture perceived to be reality by management.

UNBEACH

ATTENTIVE
LISTENING

Encourage communication.

Take input seriously—particularly from those "closest to the valve."
The people in the trenches have a perspective that needs to be
heard and understood.

One of the best communication outlets I have implemented at
companies are informal happy hours. It is amazing what everyone
learns when you get a VP sitting across from an hourly worker
over a beer, talking about the way things really are.

**Solicit and reward honest feedback
that makes the company better.**

BEACHED

SKIMP ON TECHNOLOGY
(Trip over Dollars to Pick up Pennies)

A few years ago, an engineer at a company told me he would "probably not be issued a cell phone and if he were, it most certainly would not be a smart phone." Let me get one thing straight. There is only one kind of phone, a smart phone. This would be like telling a groundskeeper he will not be issued a lawn mower, but if he were, it most certainly will not be a gas-powered mower. Smart phones are table stakes, and the only kind of phone you should own in the first place.

To not provide technology to knowledge workers is lunacy.

Another team that relies heavily on news, quotes, updates, financial data, and more was told they did not need an iPad. The irony is the company would gladly pay for them to attend a very expensive conference but didn't see the value in making it easier for them to ingest important information on a daily basis.

UNBEACH

INVEST IN TECHNOLOGY

This doesn't necessarily mean you buy the latest shiny everything (Actually, why wouldn't you?!) It does mean you invest heavily in technology and look for ways to use it to your advantage.

- Highlight new technologies at weekly meetings

- Hold classes on how to get the most out of efficiency apps

- Provide an app budget, etc.

Cell phones, tablets, and computers are the cost of doing business in today's world. Make the most of all the amazing tools available to drive communication and productivity.

BEACHED

MAKE PEOPLE BEG FOR WHAT THEY NEED

There is a common strategy around many companies characterized by the phrase, "If you want the cat, ask for the pony." This is a terrible philosophy that encourages a dishonest inflation of what is needed. Managers who want $50,000 for a particular project will request $100,000 in hopes that they will receive the needed amount.

This is corporate game playing and is not conducive to success at a company.

Managers inflate budgets knowing they are going to be arbitrarily cut to meet some magic number.

UNBEACH

ENCOURAGE AUTHENTICITY AND MEET NEEDS

Hire people you trust and who perform at a high level.

Then, if they ask for a cat, give them a cat. If they ask for a pony, give them a pony. Like the sign at many buffets, only take the food you are going to eat.

Eliminate hoarding by ensuring that people will receive what they need when they need it. If you are the keeper of the "animals," do your best to give your trusted and valued employees the animal they want and need.

Encourage a culture of authenticity and strive to be authentic yourself.

BEACHED

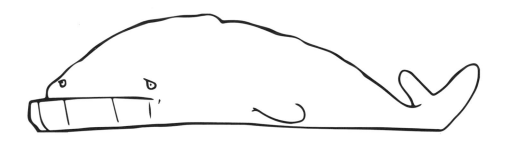

SAY ONE THING, DO ANOTHER

BW companies rarely deliver on their promises (if they make promises at all). They speak in vagaries, avoid specifics, and generally don't do what they say they are going to do.

I encouraged one manager to quit saying "we'll look into that" because that phrase had become synonymous with "you will never hear anything back on this."

Trust is very low in BW companies.

UNBEACH

ACTIONS
MATCH WORDS

When you say something, mean it.

Promises should be money in the bank.

You are as good as your word, and you want your word to be trusted, counted on, and dependable. Rather than saying, "I will look into it," describe how you will look into it. For example, "I will call our accounting department and find out what the status is. I will have a specific answer for you by Friday. Does that work for you?" Do what you say and say what you do—always.

This theory applies to your individual life as well. Watch your personal credibility grow by adopting this one trait. Be reliable. Mean what you say and say what you mean. Over deliver.

BEACHED

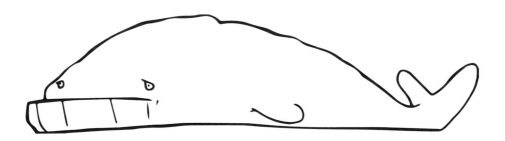

AMBIGUOUS AMBIGUITY

BW companies thrive on ambiguity. In low-accountability cultures, no one wants to be pinned down, and they cooperate by not holding anyone else accountable.

Phrases like "we're working on it," "I'll get that to you soon," and "we're making progress" are frequent responses in meetings and hallways without ever being questioned for actual metrics.

Action items come up in meetings, but no specific person is assigned ownership nor are parameters set. Instead, there is the global phrase of "we need to work on that."

UNBEACH

MEASURABLE METRICS

Make sure that every time a significant issue is discussed, an owner is assigned and a specific time frame is set. Do not accept vague, non-specific responses to requests for updates to be uttered. Make time frames, metrics, and measurable deliverables the rule of the day.

Clarity, clarity, clarity.

Establish clarity around your personal and professional values as an individual and also as the leader inside any organization.

TOP TEN ISSUES MEETING

Acting as the Change Leader for a major SAP implementation years ago, one of my responsibilities was to facilitate the meeting to discuss the top ten issues on the project with all the business leaders. In one of these meetings, one of the business leaders asked about the progress of a particular part of the project. The project manager said, "We are working on it." Knowing this was a bit ambiguous, I pushed for a more specific progress update.

Me: "I'm not sure what 'working on it' means. What kind of time frame are we looking at before we have an answer… two weeks? Four weeks…?"

Project Manager: "We are working on it. Move on."

Me: "That's really vague. Can you give the business leader a sense of where we are on this deliverable? Are we 30% complete, 50% complete…?"

Project Manager: "We are working on it. Move on!"

Me: "I'm not trying to be obstinate but that is really unclear…"

Project Manager: "G*ddammit! I said MOVE ON!"

We did move on.
Following the meeting, I closed the door behind me to the Project Manager's office and told him that better not EVER happen again.

BEACHED

BROKE, BROKE, BROKE

You see broken everywhere. Machines, computers, and equipment that don't work or are substandard fill the offices of BW companies. While interviewing people in the field, there were many complaints about equipment not working. I mentioned this to management, and they said, "If the employee's expectation is that all of the equipment will work all of the time, we can't meet that."

My question was, "Why not?"

I then asked, "Which major appliance in your house is okay to be out of commission for 6 months?"

UNBEACH

FIX IT!

Up-to-date, efficient, and functional equipment are the baseline expectation at a high-performing company.

Tools are vital to the success of any business, and excellent tools help foster excellent performance.

Are you a solution provider? Is your organization poised to solve problems? Being an individual focused on providing solutions will draw people inside and outside of the organization to you. BW companies are filled with BW leaders. Don't be one of them. Be a high-performing leader who inspires others.

THE TOILET

I was about to enter a bathroom at a client company but hesitated when I heard running water.

Assuming it was the sink, I decided to wait. The person at the close-by desk said, "I don't believe anyone is in there."

I commented on the water running. She replied, "The toilet has been running continuously for a month. We've put in 3 work orders but haven't had anyone come by to fix it."

The toilet, yes, I timed it, would flush and refill every twenty seconds.

At an estimated half gallon for each flush, that comes out to 64,800 gallons a month.

I'm sure the water company appreciated the contributions.

BEACHED

TWO VERY DISTINCT AND DIFFERENT CULTURES

BW companies have a stated culture that can be found on the lobby's wall and on the company website.

They also have a vastly different hidden culture.

The hidden culture is the way things really operate.

For example, your company says they are "pay for performance," but in reality, it is all about favoritism. The company proclaims to welcome innovation and new ideas but then shuts them down at every opportunity.

UNBEACH

ONE CULTURE

**Make sure the words
on the wall mean something.**

Truly live by the values you claim direct your company...
even when it hurts.

If you say you value customers as partners, don't do things
that would result in a breakup in any other relationship.

Measure employees at every level based on their adherence
to and manifestation of the values your company embraces
and proclaims.

BEACHED

SUPPORT A CLIMATE OF CRITICISM AND BACK BITING

BW companies are rife with critical, snarky, nasty, and gossipy communication. People talk negatively about each other to interested parties on a regular basis.

People talk behind other people's backs within the company as if they were on opposite sides of the playing field and not as if they are playing on the same team.

Zinger emails rife with derision, and attacks are viewed as "passionate involvement."

UNBEACH

INSIST ON RESPECT AS THE ONLY ACCEPTABLE CODE OF CONDUCT

When dealing with other people connected to the company, utmost respect and care should be a term of employment for everyone in the company.

Regardless of the person's position or rank, have zero tolerance for bullying and unprofessional communication. Insist on value and reward positive communication.

This does not mean that there is not ideological disagreement. It means that even ideological debate is handled in a professional manner.

Elegant leaders use respect as a communication tool and are the foundation of healthy organizations.

BEACHED

NEGATIVITY IS THE PREVAILING ATTITUDE

In BW companies, negativity is the air breathed. It is palpable as you walk around the halls, see the dour looks on people's faces, and hear the constant disgruntlement and complaining.

New opportunities are greeted with a barrage of why they will never work or will not be maintained even if they do. The general disposition toward the company and the future is one of negativity and doubt.

UNBEACH

POSITIVITY
PREVAILS

Create a company that is swimming in positivity and an upbeat atmosphere.

Create an environment where interactions are cheerful and enthusiastic. Perpetuate an energy that pulses in the air and creates an enticing atmosphere for collaboration, creativity, and success.

Starter Kit

1. Make *How to Win Friends and Influence People* by Dale Carnegie required reading

2. Make PMA (Positive Mental Attitude) part of the job expectation

3. Hire positive people

4. Create a positive environment

BEACHED

POLICY
TRUMPS PEOPLE

"The policy states…" is a phrase often uttered around a BW company. Legacy policies that make no sense for the current environment continue to be enforced like some archaic law passed to prevent horse and buggies from accessing certain parts of town or to keep women from wearing pants.

BW companies insist on ironclad compliance while refusing to examine the values or benefits of such policies.

UNBEACH

PEOPLE TRUMP POLICY

As Jesus said, "The Sabbath was created for man, and not man for the Sabbath."

Examine policies regularly to see if they're meeting the needs of your people and furthering your cause.

If they're not, adjust them or eliminate them.

Commit to "People over Policy" as your company's philosophy.

PENNY WISE, POUND FOOLISH

A long time employee, who was considered to be a highly valued leader and on the short list for promotion, was told that he owed the company $4000 for a mistake that had taken place in interpreting policy two years prior.

He was told to either pay it back or risk termination.

This single act turned a current and future thought leader for the company into a reluctant and disgruntled skeptic. Because he no longer trusted the company, he quietly rescinded any future leadership positions where he could have had a profound impact.

SCORE: Strict Adherence to Policy: 1

           Success of the Company: −10

(You have NO idea how far I had to go to get this fixed!)

BEACHED

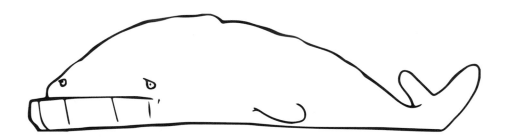

STAY IN YOUR COMFORT ZONE

At BW companies, people are encouraged to **" play it safe "** and not take risks.

They are encouraged to … **" stay off the radar, "**

" don't make waves, "

" blend in. "

They swim in a sea of mundane monotony, afraid to

COLOR OUTSIDE THE LINES.

UNBEACH

OBLITERATE
COMFORT ZONES

Understand that the comfort zone is the death zone.

You don't accomplish amazing things by playing it safe.

Inspire, encourage, and reward innovative and "out of the comfort zone" thinking!

"Unless you walk out into the unknown, the odds of making
a profound difference in your life are pretty low."

— **Tom Peters**

MAKE SURE YOUR COMFORT ZONE IS NOT SMALLER THAN THE ACTUAL SAFETY ZONE.

The brilliant Seth Godin points out the difference between your **COMFORT ZONE** and your **SAFETY ZONE**.

" Many things people view as outside of their comfort zone including public speaking, speaking up in a meeting, asking for what you want, and taking the lead are not the LEAST bit dangerous. "

BEACHED

BUDGETS, BUDGETS, BUDGETS

BW companies have the tail wagging the dog. They're all about the budget and staying within the budget, no matter what the circumstances or opportunities are. While budgets matter, they're not the purpose of any business.

In BW companies, opportunities with huge and guaranteed ROIs are passed over because they're "not in the budget." BW companies are more focused on saving money than making money.

BW companies unknowingly pass over a guaranteed 10x return because some bean counter says it is "not in the budget."

UNBEACH

FOCUS ON
RESOURCES

Understand the map is not the territory.

Budgets provide direction and discipline, but they are subservient to the needs and opportunities of the business thriving.

Foster a sense of cost consciousness, while at the same time recognizing and acting with the conviction that saving money is secondary to making money.

Make sound financial decisions that include being willing to blow the budget if big gains are available.

BEACHED

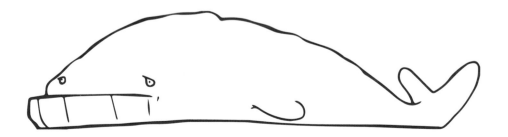

POCKET VETO'S OVERRIDE

I first heard this term when working for a very large company. We had just come out of an executive meeting with all the heavy hitters where a key decision had been made and voted on.

As we left, one of the executives asked one of the most influential members what he thought of the decision. He just shook his head and gave a slight frown. That was all it took.

The proposed plan of action would not move forward. A confidante told me that kind of "overriding" of public decisions happened all the time.

He called it... the "pocket veto."

UNBEACH

PIPE UP OR PIPE DOWN

The so-called "pocket veto" should NEVER be allowed to happen in a highly functioning organization. There is no single vote with the authority to silently override a decision, no matter how much clout the leader has.

Make sure important decisions are made and verbalized in public forums.

If a change is needed, it should occur with the same transparency.

BEACHED

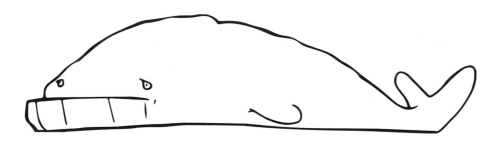

APPLAUD ACTIVITY
(NO MATTER HOW USELESS IT IS)

Busy, busy, busy.

In BW companies, activity of any kind is viewed as positive. No matter how useless or meaningless the activity, it is met with a nod of approval. As long as you are in motion you are considered to be "working," even if your activity is producing nothing of substance or value.

" In the absence of clearly defined goals, we become strangely loyal to performing daily trivia until ultimately we become enslaved by it."

—Robert Heinlein

UNBEACH

DON'T JUST DO SOMETHING, STAND THERE!

Do NOT reward activity.

Reward:
- Outcome
- Progress
- Meaningful Performance.

Being busy just to be busy should be frowned upon.

It's better to spend a day staring off into space and then generate a business changing idea than to clutter the day with trivial activity that produces no significant results.

153

BEACHED

MEDIOCRITY MALAISE

Managers hire mediocre employees because they will not make them or the team "look badly." BW managers prefer humdrum performers over rock stars, even though the rock stars outpace their teammates. "Good enough" is the job description that produces mediocre results. Mediocrity always hires mediocrity.

It is said...

A players hire A players

B players hire C players

C players hire F players

UNBEACH

HIRE THE CREAM OF THE CROP

A company is only as good as the caliber of its people. Only hire top performers and you will never have to worry about your company performing at a top level. Shun mediocrity.

*"*The best executive is one who has sense enough to pick good people to do what he wants them to do, and self-restraint enough to keep from meddling with them while they do it.*"*

—Theodore Roosevelt

BEACHED

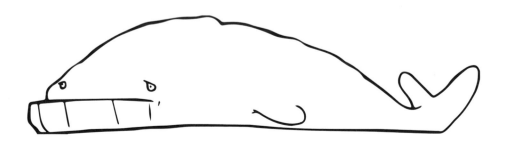

ARROGANCE ABOUNDS

BW companies have a certain cocky swagger to them. After all, they are whales. They're big and powerful, The Queen of the Ocean. They scoff at upstart competitors believing that their company is untouchable, unsurpassable, and bullet proof.

It is reported that when the subject of Netflix came up, a former senior executive of Blockbuster said:

" They're nobody."

Oops!

UNBEACH

HUMILITY
OVER HUBRIS

Recognize that no matter how dominant you currently are in your industry, your dominance can change in a heartbeat. Celebrate and build on your current success while continually reinventing your company and expanding and improving your core deliverables.

There is a reason the phrase **"Oh how the mighty have fallen"** came into existence. Pride definitely comes before a fall. Here are a few examples of dominant companies being eclipsed and overtaken.

MySpace ⟶ Facebook   Blockbuster ⟶ Netflix

Kmart ⟶ Walmart   Our Company ⟶ **Who?**

BEACHED

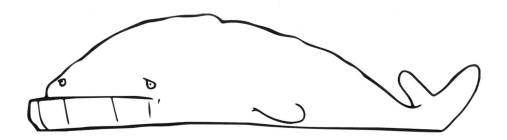

FEAR DOMINATES

BW companies are riddled with a culture of fear.

People are afraid to speak up, to sound the alarm,
or to suggest alternative courses of action.

This fear is evidenced by the blank stares in meetings,
and the uneasiness that occurs when things get a little bit
off the normal course.

In BW companies, people talk about their jobs and future
with the company in ominous tones with a lack of certainty
concerning their future.

ANNIHILATE ANXIETY

Build a spirit of adventure and advancement.

Encourage progressive thinking and new ideas, no matter how random and bizarre they may seem. Create a culture where trying something new is applauded and celebrated with gusto! The below quote from Watson about IBM is great with the exception that trying something new should never be an act of putting one's "head on the block."

Be committed to eliminating fear within yourself, your heart, your mind, and the organization you work in. It's a daily process.

" Every time we've moved ahead in IBM, it was because someone was willing to take a chance, put his head on the block, and try something new. "   —Thomas J. Watson

BEACHED

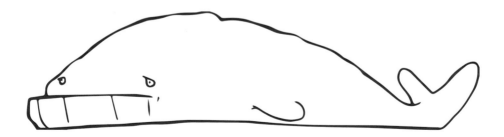

TALL POPPY SYNDROME

The Tall Poppy Syndrome is an Australian concept. It's a negative reference to people who have truly excelled or accomplished greatness but are chopped down by the jealous majority.

In BW companies, top performers are viewed as overly ambitious or "suck ups" and are pulled down and resented at every turn.

In BW companies, you want to avoid being too successful or ambitious lest jealousy erupts and you get taken down.

UNBEACH

TALL POPPIES INSPIRE MORE TALL POPPIES

Promote and celebrate top achievers.

Look for opportunities to celebrate the successes of those who are forging new paths and moving the company forward. Particularly value those who achieve with a spirit of humility and collaboration and who bring many others along with them.

Create a culture where celebrating others becomes a daily standard that is witnessed by everyone at all levels.

Practice this trait individually and organizationally—personally and professionally. Inspire, inspire, inspire!

BEACHED

LIVE THROUGH THE REARVIEW MIRROR

BW companies live in the past with very little anticipation of the future.

Past accolades and accomplishments are the clouds they ride with constant references to what we did back when.

Nostalgia and stories of the "good old days" dominate.

The focus is very much on "Look what we did…" vs. "Look what we are doing!"

UNBEACH

FUTURE FACING

Past accomplishments are great fuel for future success.
Make sure to not get stuck in the past.

The path is forward.

"No one will thank you for taking care of the present
if you have neglected the future."

—**Joel Barker**

BEACHED

RULE WITH AUTHORITY

BW companies are all about organizational charts, hierarchy, and positions. They have a "might is right" culture where your order in the food chain makes your opinion the ruling one.

Leaders have a "because I said so" mentality, which is seldom questioned by the "rank and file."

LEAD WITH INFLUENCE

Influence trumps authority every time. Evaluate ideas, proposals, and paths forward based on their merits, not based on who is presenting them. Leaders lead by influence, not authority. They gain the respect of the people they work with based on their integrity.

CONSIDER: Is it possible to have
high influence and
low authority?

Is it possible to have
high authority and
low influence?

BEACHED

THE WORLD IS LIMITED

BW companies only see their own backyard. They think the world is small; their customers are specific and few. They see no value in expanding their horizons, looking outside their borders, and going boldly where there company has not gone before.

Comfort is key, and they choose to surround themselves with people who are just like them.

UNBEACH

THE WORLD
IS FLAT

The world is indeed your oyster. Markets are emerging and opening up at dizzying speeds. Geography is shrinking as the digital world creates a previously unheard of access.

ARE YOU DOING BUSINESS IN...

China

Thailand

Dubai

Holland

Argentina

England...?   ...WHY NOT?

IF YOU ARE A BEACHED COMPANY, YOU DO NOT HAVE TO STAY THERE!

NET/NET

THE FATE OF COMPANIES THAT DON'T GET OFF THE BEACH

Like a beached whale, they may retain their shape for a long time, but slowly they rot and are picked apart. A skeleton may actually remain, but it's a mere shadow of the company that once was.

Back from the Brink...A Story of Escaping the Beach

Apple is one of the most valuable companies in history. The company famous for its cool, easy-to-use computers fell on hard times; however, in 1997, Steve Jobs came back to the company he had cofounded to try to unbeach it. Apple was suffering, posting a dozen years of losses. Jobs successfully unbeached Apple, returning it to the ocean with a string of iconic products from the iPod to the iPhone to the iPad. Steve Jobs died. It's up to Apple's new management to try to keep Jobs' juggernaut going.

UNBEACH

ANY COMPANY,

beached or not, can learn to swim
in the new ocean. To do so, however,
requires tenacity, honesly about where
the company currently is, and transparency.

As a leader and human yourself, it's your
role to ask yourself how you can make
an even bigger difference.

- **What's my contribution to the success of this organization?**

- **How can I be a conduit for progressive thinking?**

THIS BOOK IS A CATALYST TO

IGNITE
CHANGE,

AND ONE THAT
**EVERY MEMBER
OF YOUR TEAM**
SHOULD READ THIS YEAR.

NOW, GET STARTED...

1. Do a thorough assessment of your current status with your blinders off.

2. Listen. Listen. Listen. To people at all levels of your company. Check your defensiveness at the door.

3. Find out where the gaps are between your stated culture and your hidden culture. Get to what the military calls the "ground truth."

4. Stop lying to yourself and each other about the true state of the company.

5. Forge a path forward.

MY NAME IS
DR. DAREN MARTIN.

I am the Culture Architect and an expert at Unbeaching companies.

In addition to this book, I am the author of *A Company of Owners*, *Whiteboard*, and *The Sink*, and am a frequent keynote speaker at conferences.

My extensive work with Fortune 500 companies in a wide range of industries, improving worldwide organizations, and advancing a plethora of small businesses has provided an outstanding education on the changes companies need to make to perform at their peak capabilities.